Bob Lucky

CONVERSATION STARTERS IN A LANGUAGE NO ONE SPEAKS:

Excerpts from 29 Books You'll Never Read

SurVision Books

First published in 2018 by
SurVision Books
Dublin, Ireland
www.survisionmagazine.com

Copyright © Bob Lucky, 2018

Design © SurVision Books, 2018

ISBN: 978-1-912963-00-3

This book is in copyright. No part of this publication may be reproduced, stored in a retrieval system or transmitted in any form or by any means without the prior permission in writing from the publisher.

Acknowledgements

Grateful acknowledgement is made to the editors of the following, in which a number of these poems, or versions of them, originally appeared:

Shot Glass Journal: "It's so hot beer," "The man in front of me holds a box"
KYSO Flash: "There's a cloud," "No doubt this would be a good walk"
Modern Haiku: "Once the screw comes loose"

CONTENTS

No doubt this would be a good walk	4
Every time I go	5
I'm telling you the memory of the other you	6
It's so hot beer	7
This humidity	8
I've been walking	9
The House of Beer	10
I walk past my death	11
There's a cloud	12
Horror movie squeak	13
Praying	14
The man in front of me holds a box	15
The noise of the city wraps us	16
This is the sound	17
Dear Afrizal	18
My horse refused	19
There's no haiku	20
We say so many things	21
Just as I get to the intersection	22
Adam dreams	23
Every Sunday	24
Jesus walked into my dream	25
The sunlight on	26
Where did you come from?	27
I remember	28
When it's dark I don't worry	29
I was pruning my wish list	30
My father taught me three lesson	31
Once the screw comes loose	32

No doubt this would be a good walk

for a day into town. The first thing I did was pee in the bidet. That was because I stepped on my glasses getting out of bed. I noticed my left foot was bleeding. That was probably from a shard from the coffee mug I dropped on the kitchen floor. I need to check the expiration dates on the milk more often. As I was bandaging my foot with paper towels and duct tape, I toppled over and struck my head on the edge of the coffee table. Just above the right eye. There was blood everywhere but at least the roll of paper towels was at hand. Without warning, while I was dabbing the wound, I remembered the Spanish word for baby scallops – *zamburiñas*, or something that sounds like that. I'm not sure memories even exist unless you remember them. It's like a conjuring trick. But scallops must be proof of something.

from The Chronicles of Homo Hapless

Every time I go

to your place I get lost. I like getting lost. Hanging out in shops until the rain gives up with a sigh. Buying things I don't need but only if they're cheap. I have a lot of pens that don't work and candy that smells worse than medicine. Every time I go to your place I get lost. Roads hijack me at intersections. The way it used to be always lures me down a just-

lit alley. Venereous cheap beer and Kretek smoke. Fumbling for a condom and a few crumpled bills. I haven't been to your place in a long time.

from A Brief History of Excuses

I'm telling you the memory of the other you

is like a maraschino cherry hanging out inside of me forever. I knotted the stem with my teeth and tongue and spit it out on the table. The table is still here. The chair she sat on wobbles now. This morning on the toilet I was thinking. Reckoning with life expectancy averages and a bad egg. Perhaps. It's possible

she'll be with me long after I'm gone. Who was the first boy to see you naked. When it mattered. I was afraid to show my penis to anyone. It ached to be seen. When it mattered. Now with you my future smells of those small pecan pies my grandmother let me eat for breakfast. Grandmothers don't care because they love you so much. I'll never love you that much.

from Codicil to Will: The Art of Changing Your Mind

It's so hot beer

bottles sweat all over the table. Puddles join up on the tabletop to form watering holes for flies. Three wise women fan themselves with laminated menus. Nothing on the menu is available. Just a sultry breeze. Sweaty beers. Legs glisten in a blinking neon light. A local man leans over. Says slowly, we call them Butterflies. Of. The. Night. Isn't that a moth, I ask. Everyone speaks the same language differently. Tell me,

I say. I've sweated through everything – this notebook, a book of Malna's poems, my camera bag, my shirt, my underwear, my shorts, my socks, my shoes. At the edge of the Monkey Forest watching frangipani blossoms drop like gum wrappers onto the surface of a lotus pond, I was robbed by a monkey. I'm licking the sweat off my own brow. Off your brow. I can't see. Some monkey is wearing my glasses. What do you call me?

Hot
Blind
Both
More of the above

from Conversation Starters in a Language No One Speaks

This humidity

is for the birds my mother might say. Meaning she doesn't like it. Some phrases aren't as clear. As if the god of grammarians, Ganesha, the Chomsky of his day, had blown his trunk into the tissue of semantics and logic and empirical evidence. As if words meant something else entirely. A grandchild fresh out of the tub is wet as a lizard. A suntanned child is brown as a berry. My father said I was useless

as tits on a boar hog. I know what he meant. I enter the morning like a coconut falling from a tree. Life is hard. Sand only looks soft. Later I find my mind under the bed. I've read we spend 15 months of our lives looking for lost items. That's a chunk of mindlessness. I enter the morning like an egg hits a hot skillet and then devour myself. By evening I have my appetite back but can't find my mouth.

from The Real Meaning of Lost and Found

I've been walking

all day. The streets of Solo take my feet for a stroll. The streets of Solo follow me whichever way I turn. Herd me. Blisters mate with blisters. The streets of Solo frog-march me

down alleys. Songbirds in cages herald my approach and lament my passing. I smell like *turis goreng*. I can't stop even when people are taking my picture. I need to look like I know where I'm going. I've been walking all day. The air-conditioned malls are far apart. Sunset arrives like a truck hauling chickens running a red light. I know where I'm going but don't know how to get there. The streets of Solo have stolen my hotel.

from Tourist Goreng

The House of Beer

has no beer. I go to Candi Ceto. Hindu fertility temple up a winding mountain road. Tea plantations and onion fields. Greening and growing. Fertility is wasted on me. Sex at my age is recreational. I like exercise. Up the steps we climb. Click a photo of a blackened lingam. How many hands have stroked that hard rock cock and gone home to make a baby? How many babies can conceive the writhing dreams their parents braided in the darkness? On the road I pass a flattened cobra. Where are the eggs? The eggs. I don't like snakes but sometimes dream of eggs. Little snake heads poking out of shells. A cold beer would be nice. A cold shower.

from On the Uses of Desire

I walk past my death

every afternoon on my way home. Red mannequin second floor window. Naked. Sometimes I walk right below it but on sunny days I cross the street to walk in the shade. There's no vagina to speak of, which is annoying. I want to make love to my death. Red mannequin second floor window. I want to possess my death. Talk dirty. Cunt. Tits. Do not go gentle into my red death mannequin. My wife doesn't like slang words for body parts. No pussy. No boobs. It's like a doctor's examination. I palpate her breasts. Mammary intercourse. But I don't think about my red mannequin death when I get home. My wife straddles my face and says *Kiss it. Gently.* I know what *it* is.

from Temporary Immortality

There's a cloud

the color of confusion hanging over the street like a cartoon bubble full of question marks and exclamation marks. I'm having coffee with my friends and nibbling on fried tempeh. It's too hot for conversation so we just say things to keep the silence company. No one's stupid, I say, we're just all ignorant. Swastika. Not that one. Probably disagrees because he thinks I'm stupid for always paying for everyone's coffee. There's a cloud the color of rain hanging over the city like a broken promise. Hadi, the taxi driver, may be the smartest. At least he knows all the shortcuts and which times of day to avoid which intersections. Says, people believe what they can't prove and then use that belief to disprove what other people believe. There's a cloud the color of suspended disbelief hanging over the table like a poem by Emily Dickinson. Nyoman believes facts are like cockroaches. Ugly. Scurrying over countertops tabletops desktops mountaintops. Everyone wants to kill them. How do you kill a cockroach, Swastika asks rhetorically, stomp crunch stomp crunch. No no, Hadi says, don't feed it not even one crumb of thought and it will die

under the weight of opinion. Even though the coffee is so-so we order more.

from The Field Guide to Confusion

Horror movie squeak

of hinges on a heavy door. Worn brake pads. And frogs in a croaky chorus stop and start with the precision and unpredictability of Viennese neo-Nazi choirboys at a bakery window. I'm waiting for the silence to bring my dreams. I leave some lights on. The one in the hallway. The bare bulb porch light. Silence has more strength than a stork. More presence than Santa. But it's afraid of the dark. When I close my eyes I see Marcel Marceau tangoing his wallet beyond the grasp of a dance-hall butterfly of the night. I lie still and hold my breath so no one can steal it.

from Side Effects May Include Death

Praying

is like talking. To yourself. Talking. To yourself. Is not like praying. My arm is sore from strumming ukulele for three hours. I'm moving it around like a losing boxer in the twelfth round. Still thinking I've got one miracle left. The woman behind the counter thinks I'm a Stop & Go Romeo trying to put a move on her. There are cameras, you know, she says. Turn them off, I command her. If anyone ever sees me I'll lose all my powers, all my omnipotence. Don't talk dirty to me, she says. I get down on my knees.

from How to Start a Religion

The man in front of me holds a box

of disposable diapers under one arm and a six-pack of IPA in his other hand. I too have a six-pack of IPA. The line is slow. Bored, I try to be friendly. We talk about IPA for a while. The line inches forward. I'm tired of hoppiness, I say. Seems the world has gone IPA crazy. Then why are you buying that IPA, he asks. Well, I say, my taste buds are addicted. Everything else tastes like water. He smiles and puts his beer and diapers on the conveyer belt. Why are you buying those diapers, I ask.

from The After-church Crowd Swarms the Free Cheese Samples

The noise of the city wraps us

in silence. Sound waves thunder and pop like sheet-metal flags in a hurricane. My friend doesn't talk to me anymore. It's too hard. Streetlamps buzz and crackle. Words form inside us like perfect imitation pearls. We want to give them away but the time is never right. As good as tumors. Speed bumps on a neural pathway. The hum ho-hum of every night market choked with satay smoke. When I kiss her it's like speaking in tongues. I think she's trying to tell me something but the words taste meaningless. Which just adds to the noise.

from Recipes with Unknown Ingredients

This is the sound

of nostalgia trying to swallow the dry cracker of disappointment. Key lime tart doesn't taste like the memory of key lime tart. One should order something else after 20 years. This is the sound of desire trying to seduce a wrinkled passion fruit. There's a movie in my head. The soundtrack runs like a train in one ear and out the other. Locomotive gamelan. My tongue has memorized the dialog. These are the wrong lines. Limes. Key lime tart doesn't taste like the memory of key lime tart. There's not much time left. Another 20 years. I plan to devote myself to analyzing the dreams of key lime tarts. I could be a hero, academically speaking. A cymbal, this is the sound of.

from The Grant Proposal

Dear Afrizal,

Every time I see a sandal in the road, a shoe on the roof of a schoolhouse, a baby shoe in a flotsam island of trash in a canal, a high-heeled shoe wedged into a storm grate. I write you a letter. One drawer in the desk is filled with letters to you. If I knew where to send them I probably wouldn't because I like rereading them. Pretending that they're letters you wrote to me has increased the occurrences of blue moons this year. Meteorologists now have something to do besides lick a finger and stick it out the window. I like the letter about the cowboy boot in the mailbox. I put it there myself to give me something to do. The letter doesn't mention that.

from Notes from the Dead Letter Office

My horse refused

to turn left. I tried to determine the cause of this aberration for years but with no success. Her left eye was as good as the right, her left legs as good as the right. She was a stubborn creature of habit, a mule-minded beast in the body of a horse. I was slow to learn that going straight to take advantage of the shortest distance between two points is a mathematical maxim that applies mostly to birds and things not visible to the naked eye. To go left, and eventually I would have to, I had to turn right, turn right, and turn right again. When that horse died, I was lost.

from Even Though I Can't Remember the Color of the Horse

There's no haiku

large enough to house comfortably *bunga bangkai*, corpse flower, the *amorphophallus titanium* with its huge inflorescence. Even bougainvillea is a little cramped. And if the pileated woodpecker were able to

squeeze in, what decent-sized oak could you shove through the bathroom window of the caesura? What would that woodpecker peck? And without a few carpenter ants crawling around, it might starve. When the clouds gather things get messy. And the stink!

from The Problem with Haiku

We say so many things

that mean something we don't know. We don't know so many things. But we say something

anyway. Death is like that. I don't like liver but ordered it once in Lisbon because I didn't know that *fígado de frango com batatas* didn't meant 'battered chicken strips' and I was hungry and adventurous to the point that I pointed randomly at an item on the menu. I'll never forget what *fígado* means. Maybe death is like that. I liked the potatoes.

   from When I'm Gone Am I Really Somewhere Else?

Just as I get to the intersection

where I can jog to the right for a coffee or go straight to continue the self-flagellation of exercise, I'm attacked by a pack of Chihuahuas. There are five

or six of them, at least a couple. It's all a blur of bug-eyes and fangs. One of them sinks his little teeth so deep into my right calf that I scream and start waving down traffic, but the light has changed and everyone has different reasons to ignore me. My scream scares off the other attackers. So there I am with a Chihuahua clamped onto my leg. I get the impression he would also run off if he weren't so buried up to his gums in me. I manage to pry him loose, and holding him tightly around the neck, take him to the local café, where we share a brownie and come to an understanding.

from Building Bridges between the Species

Adam dreams

of going back to Paradise. In this dream I'm Eve. One day he calls me into the living room and says, we're going to Paradise, pack your bags. Paradise is expensive, probably to keep people like us out, but to tell you the truth, Galveston has better views if you squint a little. If you aren't rich, Paradise is just hell. You can't even drink a cup of coffee without thinking about how many cups of coffee you could drink for the same price back home. We're down to three bottles of wine a day. Adam's going

crazy. He comes at me with a corkscrew, babbling about the big macher needing a sacrifice. I point out there isn't a volcano around I can easily throw myself into. Drown yourself, do something, he says, there's only enough money for one more of those fucking buffets. I have to set him straight about the nature of sacrifice, and not for the first time in our marriage. You need a virgin, I remind him. And he says, why

does everything cost so much.

   from Too Much Apple Pie

Every Sunday

I never go to church. I go out for breakfast. The restaurant has no name. Just a framed poster of marine fish and an African Grey in a cage on wheels. And a nice omelet. The parrot whistles and says *as-salaam-alaikum*.

Wa-alaikum-salaam I say. Does this constitute a conversation? We discussed writing a letter to Noam Chomsky but couldn't agree on what language to use. My Parrot is rudimentary. This morning I heard the old bird say

godammit. Do birds get an extra set of wings when they die?

from Cost Benefit Analysis of the Afterlife

Jesus walked into my dream

like he owned it. I have to admit, I thought he was an asshole in need of a shave and a haircut. I wanted to say something sarcastic like *welcome*, but he had already seated himself at the table and was gnawing on some fried chicken I had reheated. The audacity

was admirable, but he had not reckoned with my mother, who showed up with my father, and was determined to get this dream in order. I'm telling you, I wanted to wake up and be done with it, but I was sitting in a corner and no longer had control of anything. Next thing I know, my father is sitting next to me and complaining

about how I don't know how to cook chicken – this from a man who can't make a sandwich – and Jesus is doing the dishes. I get this warm glow because in my dream my mother is god, which means I am the son of god.

   from Divinity, or Whose Mother Isn't a Virgin?

The sunlight on

the porch. Wet every other day. That's when the gardener comes. Hoses down the porch, which then is also

slippery, slippery sunlight. Shining wetness. Wet light. My ass

has on occasion slipped on the sunlight and I've spoken to the gardener, whom I call Ayman, asking him to hose it down *after* I've gone to work. But there are problems. His conception of work and mine

aren't quite the same. And his real name is something else so it's easy for him to pretend he doesn't know

what I'm saying. Slippery is slippery.

> *from* Watering and Whacking the Weeds, My Life with Ayman, the Gardener

Where did you come from?

What do you mean? I mean, where did you come

from? From work. Not literally. Not literally? Not literally. Let me rephrase my question: Where do you come from? Does that help? I suppose

so. New York. New York? New York. Why did you come here? Everyone wants to go there. Everyone? Almost

everyone. Where are you from? Not from around here. That narrows it down to just about anywhere.

And what do you do? I sit in a dark room and calculate the many ways the Way can be calculated, and there are many ways indeed. Do you know Descartes

tried mathematically to prove the existence of God? I do. You do? I do. Then you've heard the jokes?

from What Analytical Geometry Means to Me

I remember

accidentally washing a number 2 pencil in a load of laundry and debating whether or not I should put it in the dryer. I remember

getting a hard-on, a boner, and then a harder-on, and then one day the genie came out of the bottle, and I had only three fucking wishes. I remember

blowing a couple of those.

    from Remembering Joe Brainard

When it's dark I don't worry

about the bats so much. But the birds. They heckle the sun until it sinks, drag it into the palms and peck it to

death. Gory sunset but riveting, like the *telenovela* in which the sweet matriarch is an assassin. Always cleans her mess up. Quick

with explanations. The beautiful granddaughter is catching on. One eye on the door, close to the keyhole, one hand on the *panocha*. The other hand and the other eye? That's what no one knows. Viewers tune in because the granddaughter is getting too big for her bra. Off course,

it takes their minds off the birds outside.

   from The Life of a Failed Virgin

I was pruning my wish list

one starless night when I fell in love. The pit was dark and filled with people who had been there so long their eyes no longer shone. I turned to one whose smile smelled of light. I would love to play games with you, I said, answering a question

she hadn't asked.

from Seduction, One Damn Mistake after Another

My father taught me three lessons

I failed to understand.

The swimming lesson: First I swam through the air. He grabbed an arm and a leg, twirled like a dervish discus thrower and hurled me towards the middle of the pond, where, eyes closed, I began to thrash my way back to shore guided by the sound of his laughter.

The dancing lesson: I was sitting in the bed of the pick-up truck. He threw his cigar butt out the window and into my lap. I tap-danced my way from the edge of death at 60 miles per hour. I don't think he watched much of the show, wanted me to do the Cotton-Eyed Joe. Tap dancing was for fruits.

The hitting-the-nail-on-the-head lesson: He pulled me out of the Tarzan book I was reading and into the carport, where he made me pound nails into blocks of wood. After I bent a certain number of nails, he snapped, raised his hatchet-hammer to whack me, but just then, like Tarzan to the rescue, the mailman pulled into the driveway. Special delivery.

from How to Die and Other Essential Life Skills

Once the screw comes loose,

you know. It's the classic example of foreshadowing. You wait for everything

to fall apart. Every sound becomes an omen. Shadows cross your path like herds of black cats. Sidewalks, varicose-veined with cracks daring you to break your mother's back, peter out into deserts where

cacti only promise to bloom. Every kiss is a bullet. Every glance a paper cut. But before anything happens

(a yellow post-it stuck to the computer screen)

it's too late.

from Fate Is Just Time Keeping Track of You

More poetry published by SurVision Books

Noelle Kocot. Humanity
 (New Poetics: USA)
 ISBN 978-1-9995903-0-7

Ciaran O'Driscoll. The Speaking Trees
 (New Poetics: Ireland)
 ISBN 978-1-9995903-1-4

Elin O'Hara Slavick. Cameramouth
 (New Poetics: USA)
 ISBN 978-1-9995903-4-5

Anatoly Kudryavitsky. Stowaway
 (New Poetics: Ireland)
 ISBN 978-1-9995903-2-1

Christopher Prewitt. Paradise Hammer
 (Winner of James Tate Poetry Prize 2018)
 ISBN 978-1-9995903-9-0

George Kalamaras. That Moment of Wept
 ISBN 978-1-9995903-7-6

Anton G. Leitner. Selected Poems 1981–2015
 Translated from German
 ISBN 978-1-9995903-8-3

Sergey Biryukov. Transformations
   Translated from Russian
   (New Poetics: Russia)
   ISBN 978-1-9995903-5-2

Maria Grazia Calandrone. Fossils
   Translated from Italian
   (New Poetics: Italy)
   ISBN 978-1-9995903-6-9

Our books are available to order via
http://survisionmagazine.com/books.htm

www.ingramcontent.com/pod-product-compliance
Lightning Source LLC
Chambersburg PA
CBHW061314040426
42444CB00010B/2633